The Man Caught By A Fish

THE BOOK OF JONAH FOR CHILDREN

Written by M. M. Brem

Illustrated by Jim Roberts

ARCH© Books
Copyright © 1967 Concordia Publishing House
3558 S. Jefferson Avenue, St. Louis, Mo 63118-3968
Manufactured in Colombia

When God looked down on Nineveh,
that city made Him sad
because the things its people did
were almost always bad.

"The way they live must change," God thought.
"A prophet must be sent."
So God told Jonah he should go
and tell them to repent.

But Jonah didn't want to go:
"I just can't waste my time
on strangers who don't love my Lord
and are not friends of mine.

"I just won't go to Nineveh!"
So Jonah left that day
and bought a ticket on a ship
that went the other way.

He went aboard and looked around
the inside of the ship.
"Since God won't find me here," he thought,
"I'll rest up on my trip."

But as he slept, God sent a storm
with winds that were so strong
that soon the sailors were afraid
their ship would not last long.

And as the waves became so high
that they could sink the boat,
they threw their cargo overboard
to keep their ship afloat.

But nothing helped. Then someone said,
"The storm was sent because
of something one of us has done.
To find him, let's draw straws."

And Jonah drew the shortest straw.
They asked, "Are you the one?
Has your God sent this storm on us
because of what you've done?"

And on the slippery deck he faced
the men. His face was grim.
"I tried to run away from God,
but one can't run from Him.

"I know these winds and mighty waves
were sent here by my Lord.
So if you want to stop this storm,
just throw me overboard!"

"We can't do that," they cried aloud.
They tried to row instead.
It didn't help. So in the end
they did what Jonah said.

As soon as he was overboard,
the sea was calm again,
and all the men knelt down and prayed
to God our Lord right then.

As Jonah sank beneath the waves,
he couldn't hold his breath.
But God had sent a mighty fish
to rescue him from death.

The fish swam up, mouth opened wide,
and swallowed Jonah down.
So in the belly of the fish
God didn't let him drown.

Three days and nights he cried to God
because he was afraid.
"You should have gone to Nineveh,"
God told him as he prayed.

"To you the Ninevites are strange,
but they're My people, too.
You should have brought My Word to them
as you were told to do."

And then God sent the fish toward land,
and with a mighty cough

the fish dumped Jonah on the sand
and turned and then swam off.

And Jonah knew what he must do.
He had a second chance.
He started off toward Nineveh
without a backward glance.

And when he got to Nineveh,
he preached all through the town.
"In forty days you all will die!
My God is coming down.

"You wonder why? Just look around!
You see the things you do.
And most of what you say and think
is mean and wicked, too!"

They hung their heads in shame. Some cried.
They didn't even eat.
They put on rags, took off their shoes,
and walked in their bare feet.

As God looked down, He saw their hearts
had changed. They understood.
And so He thought, "I won't destroy
them as I said I would."

Then Jonah went outside the walls
to watch the Lord come down.
"Those forty days have long since passed.
God should destroy this town!"

Now God had caused a plant to grow
to give him extra shade.
But Jonah only sat and sulked
inside the booth he'd made.

"I'll just stay here," he told himself,
"where I can watch the town."
And as he sat, he was surprised.
The leaves were falling down!

"What is the matter here?" he said.
"Now I have lost my shade."
And in the stem he saw a hole
he thought a worm had made.

He bent and looked. "I think a worm
has killed it," Jonah said.
And he was angry with the worm
because the plant was dead.

But then God came and spoke to him.
"What kind of man are you?
You feel so sorry for a plant –
why not this city, too?

"Just think how happy they must be.
Why do you have that frown?
The angels cheer when ONE is saved;
through you I saved a TOWN!"

DEAR PARENTS:

The story of the "man caught by a fish" is not just a tale about some poor fool who found out you can't run away from God and then was rescued in a fantastic way—by a huge fish. The main interest of the Book of Jonah is the pagan city of Nineveh and how God and an upright believer felt about the people there.

To a righteous Israelite like Jonah the Assyrian capital of Nineveh was just a den of wickedness, a people who did not believe in the true God. They were outsiders who in his view had no claim on the concern and compassion of those who were "in." The Ninevites were strange and morally corrupt. Why bother with them?

Yet God does not share Jonah's feelings of superiority and indifference. He is a "gracious God and merciful" (Jonah 4:2). He has "no pleasure in the death of the wicked but [desires] that he may turn [repent] from his way and live" (Ezek. 33:11). His concern and love reach far beyond the people who belong to Him already. He also has "other sheep" (John 10:16) and makes His people responsible for them.

Will you help your child see God's great love in this story? And will you help him express God's love to other people?

THE EDITOR